A+
books

Step-by-Step
Stories

Making a Jack-o'-Lantern,

Step by Step

by J. Angelique Johnson

CAPSTONE PRESS
a capstone imprint

A+ Books are published by Capstone Press,
151 Good Counsel Drive, P.O. Box 669, Mankato, Minnesota 56002.
www.capstonepub.com

 Books published by Capstone Press are manufactured with paper
containing at least 10 percent post-consumer waste.

Library of Congress Cataloging-in-Publication Data
Johnson, J. Angelique.
  Making a Jack-o'-lantern, step by step / by J. Angelique Johnson.
    p. cm. — (A+. Step-by-step stories)
  ISBN 978-1-4296-6023-5 (library binding)
  1. Halloween decorations—Juvenile literature. 2. Jack-o-lanterns—Juvenile literature. I. Title.
TT900.H32J65 2012
745.594'1—dc22

                                2011002614

Credits

Shelly Lyons, editor; Ted Williams, designer; Marcie Spence, media researcher; Sarah Schuette, photo stylist;
Marcy Morin, studio scheduler; Eric Manske, production specialist

Photo Credits

Capstone Studio: Karon Dubke, cover, 1, 4–5, 5 (inset), 7, 8 (insets), 8–9, 10–11, 12,
13, 14 (inset), 14–15, 16, 17, 18–19, 20, 21, 22, 23, 24, 25, 26, 27, 28, 29; Shutterstock:
Alita Bobrov, 6, s_oleg, cover (background)

Note to Parents, Teachers, and Librarians

Step-by-Step Stories is a nonfiction set that teaches sequencing skills along with solid information about the
title subjects. Through fun text and photos, this set supports math and science concepts such as order of
events, relative position words, and ordinal positions. Use the exercise on page 28 to help children practice
their sequencing skills.

Printed in the United States of America in North Mankato, Minnesota.
032011   006110CGF11

Table of Contents

Time to Find a Pumpkin

The leaves are changing color. The days have gotten shorter. It's fall! Now is the time to find a pumpkin.

Elliot and his father are looking for a pumpkin. They will find the perfect one to carve into a jack-o'-lantern for Halloween night.

Pumpkin seeds are planted in spring. By fall the seeds have grown into pumpkins.

There are about 30 kinds of pumpkins. They come in many shapes and sizes. They can be tiny and bumpy. Pumpkins can even be blue!

The world's largest pumpkin weighed more than 1,700 pounds (771 kilograms). That's as heavy as a small car!

6

Elliot looks for a big orange pumpkin for his jack-o'-lantern.

Elliot finds the perfect pumpkin. He looks it over. First he checks the stem. It should be at least 2 inches (5.1 centimeters) long. A short stem can lead to rotting.

Next Elliot checks the pumpkin's shell. He makes sure there are no soft spots.

Pumpkins can spoil quickly once they are picked. It's best to store them in a cool, dry place until used.

9

Getting Ready

Elliot and Dad take the pumpkin home. Before carving it, they must find the right supplies. Elliot covers a table with newspaper. He also gets soapy water, a washcloth, and a towel.

Dad looks for a long, thin knife. He grabs an ice-cream scoop, a bowl, and some tape. They will need a pattern, a pen, and a paring knife. A nail, a pumpkin-carving tool, and a pumpkin-scraping tool will also be used. And don't forget the candle!

Next Dad puts the pumpkin on top of the newspaper. He handles the pumpkin with care. Bruised pumpkins spoil quickly.

12

Then Elliot washes the shell with the washcloth. After Elliot dries the pumpkin, Dad will be ready to cut it.

13

Preparing the Pumpkin

Before cutting, Dad marks the size of the lid. It should be large enough to put a hand through. The ice-cream scoop will need to fit too. To be safe, Dad handles the knife. He cuts around the pumpkin's stem.

Next Elliot uses the ice-cream scoop. He picks out the white seeds with his fingers.

Pumpkin seeds are full of protein. They can be roasted as a snack. Yum!

16

Elliot scoops out the insides of the pumpkin. Afterward he scrapes the inside walls clean. What a mess!

When he's done, Elliot washes the shell again. Then he dries it with the towel.

17

Elliot and Dad look at the pumpkin's shell. They decide which side is best for carving. They choose the smoothest side. Now Elliot needs to pick his jack-o'-lantern design. Which pattern will he choose?

Many jack-o'-lanterns have scary faces. Some are carved into spiders and ghosts. Others spell out words like "Beware" and "Boo!"

Making the Jack-O'-Lantern

Before marking the pumpkin, Dad and Elliot tape the pattern to the shell.

Next Dad marks the pumpkin's shell with a nail. There are two eyes, a nose, and a creepy mouth. Then Elliot removes the pattern.

It's time to carve the jack-o'-lantern's face. Dad uses the carving tool. He slowly saws through the pumpkin's shell. He stays inside the marks he made.

Then Elliot uses his fingers to pull out the pumpkin pieces. He is careful not to break the shell.

Now it's time to make the jack-o'-lantern glow. First Elliot places the unlit candle inside the pumpkin.

Candles aren't the only way to make a jack-o'-lantern glow. Some people use lights that flicker and flash.

24

Uh-oh! The candle tips over.

Inside the pumpkin, the bottom is too bumpy. Elliot scrapes the bottom flat. Then the candle stands straight.

Later Elliot puts his jack-o'-lantern on the doorstep. Dad lights the candle. Soon children line the streets. They trick-or-treat and take a peek at Elliot's jack-o'-lantern.

26

Just look at it glow!

27

Mixed-up Mess!

Now that you've learned the steps in making the perfect jack-o'-lantern, can you put these pictures in order?

A Enjoy your spooky jack-o'-lantern!

B Carve the jack-o'-lantern's face.

28

D Pick the perfect pumpkin.

C Scoop out the pumpkin's slimy insides.

Glossary

carve—to slice through something

pattern—something used as a model for making things

protein—something found in all plants and animals; meat, cheese, eggs, beans, nuts, and fish are good sources of protein

shell—a hard outer covering

stem—the long main part of a plant from which leaves and flowers grow

Read More

Internet Sites

Brennan-Nelson, Denise. *J Is for Jack-o-Lantern: A Halloween Alphabet.* Chelsea, Mich.: Sleeping Bear Press, 2009.

Koontz, Robin. *Pick a Perfect Pumpkin: Learning about Pumpkin Harvests.* Autumn. Mankato, Minn.: Picture Window Books, 2010.

Rustad, Martha E. H. *Fall Pumpkins: Orange and Plump.* Cloverleaf Books. Fall's Here! Minneapolis: Millbrook Press, 2012.

FactHound offers a safe, fun way to find Internet sites related to this book. All of the sites on FactHound have been researched by our staff.

Here's all you do:

Visit *www.facthound.com*

Type in this code: 9781429660235

Super-cool stuff! Check out projects, games and lots more at **www.capstonekids.com**